EMMANUEL JOSEPH

The Technology of Longing, Nostalgia, Solitude, and the Human Quest for Connection

Copyright © 2025 by Emmanuel Joseph

All rights reserved. No part of this publication may be reproduced, stored or transmitted in any form or by any means, electronic, mechanical, photocopying, recording, scanning, or otherwise without written permission from the publisher. It is illegal to copy this book, post it to a website, or distribute it by any other means without permission.

First edition

This book was professionally typeset on Reedsy.
Find out more at reedsy.com

Contents

1	Chapter 1: The Digital Age and the Birth of Longing	1
2	Chapter 2: The Echoes of Nostalgia	3
3	Chapter 3: Solitude in the Digital Era	4
4	Chapter 4: The Human Quest for Connection	6
5	Chapter 5: The Evolution of Communication	8
6	Chapter 6: The Impact of Social Media	10
7	Chapter 7: The Role of Virtual Reality	12
8	Chapter 8: The Intersection of Technology and Emotion	14
9	Chapter 9: The Role of Artificial Intelligence	16
10	Chapter 10: The Future of Connection	18
11	Chapter 11: The Human Touch in a Digital World	19
12	Chapter 12: The Role of Community	21
13	Chapter 13: The Role of Memory	23
14	Chapter 14: The Power of Storytelling	25
15	Chapter 15: The Role of Art and Creativity	27
16	Chapter 16: The Power of Music	29
17	Chapter 17: The Journey Ahead	31

1

Chapter 1: The Digital Age and the Birth of Longing

In the digital age, humanity's yearning for connection has taken on new dimensions. With the advent of social media and instant messaging, the boundaries of communication expanded, allowing people to reach out across continents. Yet, amidst this technological marvel, a paradox emerged: the more connected we became, the deeper our longing for genuine, heartfelt connections grew. The superficiality of online interactions often left individuals feeling isolated, as the screen became both a bridge and a barrier.

Nostalgia, a powerful emotional force, found fertile ground in this landscape. The memories of simpler times, when connections were forged face-to-face, began to haunt our digital existence. We reminisced about the warmth of a handwritten letter, the joy of a spontaneous visit, and the authenticity of unfiltered conversations. This longing for the past, coupled with the solitude of modern living, ignited a quest to reclaim the essence of human connection.

As we navigated the complexities of the digital world, we realized that technology could not replace the depth of human interaction. It became evident that while technology facilitated communication, it could not fulfill the inherent need for intimacy and understanding. The digital age, with all its advancements, inadvertently magnified our longing for true connection, compelling us to seek meaningful relationships beyond the confines of our screens.

2

Chapter 2: The Echoes of Nostalgia

Nostalgia, often described as a bittersweet emotion, is a testament to the enduring power of memory. In the realm of technology, nostalgia manifests itself in various forms, from the revival of vintage devices to the resurgence of retro aesthetics. This yearning for the past is not merely a longing for obsolete gadgets; it is a deeper reflection of our desire to reconnect with the emotions and experiences those devices once evoked.

The nostalgia triggered by technology is a complex interplay of past and present. It is a longing for the simplicity of earlier times, when life was less cluttered by notifications and updates. This sentiment is echoed in the resurgence of vinyl records, typewriters, and Polaroid cameras—symbols of an era when technology was less intrusive and more tangible. These relics of the past evoke a sense of comfort and familiarity, reminding us of the joy found in the analog world.

However, nostalgia is not just about reclaiming the past; it is also a response to the challenges of the present. In a world saturated with information, where every moment is documented and shared, the authenticity of personal experiences often feels compromised. The technology of longing compels us to seek refuge in memories, to find solace in the simplicity and genuineness of bygone days. Nostalgia becomes a coping mechanism, allowing us to navigate the complexities of the digital age with a sense of continuity and connection.

3

Chapter 3: Solitude in the Digital Era

The digital era, while fostering connectivity, has paradoxically amplified feelings of solitude. The constant barrage of online interactions, notifications, and virtual engagements can create a sense of isolation, as individuals grapple with the disparity between superficial connections and the deep human need for genuine companionship. Solitude, once a space for reflection and introspection, has morphed into an experience of digital alienation.

In the quest for connection, the solitude of the digital age often becomes overwhelming. The screen, a portal to the world, can simultaneously serve as a barrier, creating a sense of distance and disconnection. Despite the plethora of social platforms, the absence of face-to-face interactions fosters a unique form of loneliness, as the nuances of human presence are lost in translation. The technology of longing emerges as a response to this solitude, driving individuals to seek meaningful connections beyond the virtual realm.

The solitude experienced in the digital era is compounded by the curated nature of online presence. Social media, with its emphasis on perfection and projection, often leads to feelings of inadequacy and isolation. The technology of longing compels us to seek authenticity, to break free from the constraints of digital facades and embrace the imperfections of real-life interactions. In this pursuit, solitude becomes a catalyst for deeper human connections, as we strive to transcend the superficiality of online engagements and rediscover

CHAPTER 3: SOLITUDE IN THE DIGITAL ERA

the essence of companionship.

4

Chapter 4: The Human Quest for Connection

At the heart of the technology of longing lies the fundamental human quest for connection. This quest, driven by an innate desire for intimacy and understanding, has been both facilitated and hindered by technological advancements. While technology has bridged geographical distances, it has also created emotional barriers, as individuals struggle to find genuine connections amidst the cacophony of digital noise.

The human quest for connection is a journey marked by moments of solitude and nostalgia. It is a search for the warmth of human presence, the comfort of shared experiences, and the depth of authentic relationships. Technology, with all its innovations, has highlighted the importance of these connections, reminding us that true companionship cannot be replicated by virtual interactions. The longing for connection becomes a driving force, compelling us to seek out spaces where we can forge meaningful bonds.

In the pursuit of connection, we encounter the technology of longing as both a challenge and an opportunity. It challenges us to navigate the complexities of the digital world, to find balance between virtual and real-life interactions. Simultaneously, it presents opportunities to redefine our relationships, to embrace the potential of technology while honoring the essence of human connection. The quest for connection is an ongoing journey, one that requires us to reconcile the solitude of the digital age with the richness of shared experiences and the joy of genuine companionship.

5

Chapter 5: The Evolution of Communication

The evolution of communication has been a defining aspect of the technology of longing. From handwritten letters to instant messaging, the ways in which we connect have transformed, reflecting the changing dynamics of human interaction. This evolution, while enabling rapid and widespread communication, has also introduced new challenges, as the depth of personal connections often becomes compromised in the digital landscape.

In the early days of communication, the written word held immense power, as letters conveyed emotions and experiences across distances. The act of writing, with its intentionality and thoughtfulness, fostered a sense of intimacy and connection. As technology advanced, communication became more instantaneous, with the advent of telephones and emails. While these innovations bridged distances, they also altered the nature of interaction, as the immediacy of communication often overshadowed its depth.

The digital age has further accelerated this evolution, with social media and messaging apps dominating the landscape. The speed and convenience of online communication have revolutionized the way we connect, yet they have also introduced challenges, as the nuances of human presence are lost in virtual interactions. The technology of longing compels us to seek

CHAPTER 5: THE EVOLUTION OF COMMUNICATION

balance, to reclaim the authenticity of communication amidst the rapid pace of technological advancements.

In the quest for meaningful connections, the evolution of communication becomes a focal point. It reminds us that while technology can facilitate interactions, it cannot replace the depth of human presence. The technology of longing drives us to embrace both the advancements and limitations of communication, to find ways to honor the essence of connection in the digital age. Through this process, we navigate the complexities of communication, seeking to bridge the gap between virtual and real-life interactions.

6

Chapter 6: The Impact of Social Media

Social media, a cornerstone of the digital age, has profoundly influenced the technology of longing. Platforms such as Facebook, Instagram, and Twitter have revolutionized the way we connect, enabling individuals to share experiences and engage with others across the globe. However, the impact of social media on human connection is multifaceted, as it both fosters and hinders the quest for meaningful relationships.

The technology of longing is evident in the ways individuals use social media to seek connection. The act of sharing personal moments, thoughts, and feelings online reflects a desire to be seen and understood. Social media provides a platform for self-expression, allowing individuals to reach out to others and create virtual communities. Yet, amidst this connectivity, a sense of isolation often emerges, as the superficiality of online interactions can leave individuals feeling disconnected.

The curated nature of social media further amplifies the longing for genuine connections. The emphasis on perfection and projection can lead to feelings of inadequacy, as individuals compare their lives to the idealized representations of others. The technology of longing compels us to seek authenticity, to navigate the complexities of social media with a sense of intentionality and self-awareness. It drives us to find spaces where we can engage in meaningful interactions, beyond the confines of virtual facades.

CHAPTER 6: THE IMPACT OF SOCIAL MEDIA

In the impact of social media, the technology of longing becomes a catalyst for deeper human connections. It challenges us to rethink the ways we use digital platforms, to prioritize the essence of human presence amidst the cacophony of online engagements. Through this process, we navigate the complexities of social media, seeking to bridge the gap between virtual and real-life interactions, and to reclaim the depth of connection in the digital age.

7

Chapter 7: The Role of Virtual Reality

Virtual reality (VR) has emerged as a transformative technology, offering immersive experiences that redefine the boundaries of human interaction. The technology of longing finds expression in VR, as individuals seek to bridge the gap between virtual and real-life connections. VR provides a unique opportunity to explore the depths of human presence, enabling individuals to engage in shared experiences that transcend physical distances.

The role of VR in the quest for connection is multifaceted. On one hand, VR offers the potential to create meaningful interactions, as individuals can participate in virtual environments that mimic real-life experiences. This immersive technology allows for a sense of presence, enabling individuals to engage in shared activities, from virtual meetings to social gatherings. The technology of longing is evident in the ways VR is used to foster connections, creating spaces where individuals can interact in more authentic and engaging ways.

However, the impact of VR on human connection is not without challenges. The immersive nature of VR can create a sense of detachment, as individuals grapple with the disparity between virtual and real-life interactions. The technology of longing compels us to navigate these complexities, to find balance between the immersive experiences of VR and the authenticity of real-life connections. VR becomes a tool for exploration, allowing us to

CHAPTER 7: THE ROLE OF VIRTUAL REALITY

redefine the boundaries of human interaction while honoring the essence of genuine presence.

8

Chapter 8: The Intersection of Technology and Emotion

The intersection of technology and emotion is a key aspect of the technology of longing. As digital platforms and devices become integral to our lives, the ways in which we experience and express emotions are profoundly influenced. The technology of longing emerges as we navigate this landscape, seeking to reconcile the emotional depth of human experiences with the rapid pace of technological advancements.

Technology has the power to amplify emotions, as digital platforms provide spaces for self-expression and connection. Social media, messaging apps, and online communities offer opportunities to share experiences, seek support, and forge bonds. However, the technology of longing is evident in the ways these platforms can also heighten feelings of isolation, inadequacy, and disconnection. The curated nature of online presence often leads to a sense of emotional detachment, as individuals grapple with the disparity between virtual interactions and real-life emotions.

The quest for connection drives us to seek authenticity in our digital interactions, to find spaces where emotions can be expressed and understood in their full complexity. The technology of longing compels us to navigate the intersection of technology and emotion with intentionality and self-awareness, to embrace the potential of digital platforms while honoring the depth of human experiences. Through this process, we strive to create meaningful connections that transcend the superficiality of online engagements.

9

Chapter 9: The Role of Artificial Intelligence

Artificial intelligence (AI) has become a defining feature of the digital age, influencing various aspects of human life. The technology of longing finds expression in AI, as individuals seek to harness its potential to enhance human connection. AI offers unique opportunities to explore the depths of human interaction, enabling individuals to engage with technology in more personalized and meaningful ways.

The role of AI in the quest for connection is multifaceted. On one hand, AI-powered platforms and applications provide tools for communication, self-expression, and support. From chatbots to virtual assistants, AI offers opportunities to engage with technology in ways that mimic human interactions. The technology of longing is evident in the ways AI is used to foster connections, creating spaces where individuals can interact with technology in more authentic and engaging ways.

However, the impact of AI on human connection is not without challenges. The limitations of AI, such as its inability to fully replicate human emotions and experiences, create a sense of detachment. The technology of longing compels us to navigate these complexities, to find balance between the potential of AI and the authenticity of human presence. AI becomes a tool for exploration, allowing us to redefine the boundaries of human interaction

CHAPTER 9: THE ROLE OF ARTIFICIAL INTELLIGENCE

while honoring the essence of genuine connection.

10

Chapter 10: The Future of Connection

The future of connection is shaped by the technology of longing, as individuals seek to navigate the complexities of the digital age. As technology continues to evolve, the ways in which we connect will be profoundly influenced, reflecting the changing dynamics of human interaction. The technology of longing will drive us to seek meaningful connections, to find balance between virtual and real-life engagements, and to embrace the potential of technological advancements while honoring the depth of human presence.

In the quest for connection, the future will be marked by moments of nostalgia, solitude, and longing. These emotions will compel us to seek authenticity in our interactions, to navigate the complexities of digital platforms with intentionality and self-awareness. The technology of longing will become a catalyst for deeper human connections, driving us to create spaces where meaningful bonds can be forged.

The future of connection will be shaped by our ability to reconcile the potential of technology with the essence of human presence. As we navigate this landscape, the technology of longing will remind us of the importance of genuine connections, the joy of shared experiences, and the depth of authentic relationships. Through this process, we will redefine the boundaries of human interaction, seeking to create a future where technology enhances, rather than diminishes, the richness of human connection.

11

Chapter 11: The Human Touch in a Digital World

In the digital world, the human touch remains an essential element of connection. Despite the advancements in technology, the warmth of human presence, the comfort of physical touch, and the authenticity of face-to-face interactions cannot be replicated by virtual engagements. The technology of longing compels us to seek spaces where the human touch can be honored, to find ways to integrate the depth of human presence with the potential of technological advancements.

The human touch is a powerful force, one that transcends the limitations of digital platforms. It is the warmth of a hug, the reassurance of a hand on the shoulder, and the comfort of shared laughter. These moments of human presence create bonds that are both deep and enduring, fostering a sense of connection that cannot be replicated by virtual interactions. The technology of longing drives us to seek authenticity in our interactions, to find balance between the virtual and the real, and to honor the essence of human connection.

In the quest for meaningful connections, the human touch becomes a focal point. It reminds us of the importance of presence, the joy of shared experiences, and the depth of authentic relationships. The technology of longing compels us to navigate the complexities of the digital world with intentionality and self-awareness, to create spaces where the human touch can be honored and celebrated. Through this process, we seek to redefine the boundaries of human interaction, to create a future where technology enhances, rather than diminishes, the richness of human connection.

12

Chapter 12: The Role of Community

Community plays a crucial role in the technology of longing, as individuals seek to navigate the complexities of the digital age. The sense of belonging, the comfort of shared experiences, and the support of communal bonds are essential elements of human connection. The technology of longing compels us to seek spaces where communities can thrive, to find ways to foster meaningful connections that transcend the limitations of digital platforms.

Communities, both online and offline, offer opportunities for individuals to engage in shared activities, to seek support, and to forge bonds. The technology of longing is evident in the ways individuals use digital platforms to create virtual communities, spaces where they can connect with others who share similar interests and experiences. These communities provide a sense of belonging, fostering connections that are both deep and enduring.

However, the impact of digital platforms on community is not without challenges. The superficiality of online interactions, the curated nature of social media, and the sense of isolation that often accompanies virtual engagements can create barriers to genuine connection. The technology of longing compels us to navigate these complexities, to find balance between virtual and real-life interactions, and to create spaces where communities can thrive. Through this process, we seek to honor the essence of communal bonds, to foster meaningful connections that enrich our lives and enhance our sense of belonging.

13

Chapter 13: The Role of Memory

Memory plays a pivotal role in the technology of longing, as individuals seek to navigate the complexities of the digital age. The memories of past experiences, the emotions they evoke, and the connections they create are essential elements of human interaction. The technology of longing compels us to seek spaces where memories can be honored, to find ways to integrate the richness of past experiences with the potential of technological advancements.

Memory is a powerful force, one that shapes our sense of identity and connection. The memories of shared experiences, the emotions they evoke, and the bonds they create are essential elements of human interaction. The technology of longing is evident in the ways individuals use digital platforms to capture and share memories, to create virtual spaces where past experiences can be revisited and celebrated. These memories provide a sense of continuity, fostering connections that are both deep and enduring.

However, the impact of digital platforms on memory is not without challenges. The constant barrage of information, the curated nature of online presence, and the sense of detachment that often accompanies virtual engagements can create barriers to genuine connection. The technology of longing compels us to navigate these complexities, to find balance between the virtual and the real, and to create spaces where memories can be honored and celebrated. Through this process, we seek to redefine the boundaries of human interaction, to create a future where technology enhances, rather than diminishes, the richness of human connection.

14

Chapter 14: The Power of Storytelling

Storytelling is a fundamental aspect of the technology of longing, as individuals seek to navigate the complexities of the digital age. The act of sharing stories, the connections they create, and the emotions they evoke are essential elements of human interaction. The technology of longing compels us to seek spaces where storytelling can be honored, to find ways to integrate the richness of human experiences with the potential of technological advancements.

Storytelling is a powerful force, one that transcends the limitations of digital platforms. It is the act of sharing experiences, the connections they create, and the emotions they evoke that foster a sense of connection. The technology of longing is evident in the ways individuals use digital platforms to share stories, to create virtual spaces where human experiences can be captured and celebrated. These stories provide a sense of continuity, fostering connections that are both deep and enduring.

However, the impact of digital platforms on storytelling is not without challenges. The superficiality of online interactions, the curated nature of social media, and the sense of detachment that often accompanies virtual engagements can create barriers to genuine connection. The technology of longing compels us to navigate these complexities, to find balance between the virtual and the real, and to create spaces where storytelling can be honored and celebrated. Through this process, we seek to redefine the boundaries of human interaction, to create a future where technology enhances, rather than diminishes, the richness of human connection.

15

Chapter 15: The Role of Art and Creativity

Art and creativity play a crucial role in the technology of longing, as individuals seek to navigate the complexities of the digital age. The act of creating, the connections it fosters, and the emotions it evokes are essential elements of human interaction. The technology of longing compels us to seek spaces where art and creativity can be honored, to find ways to integrate the richness of human experiences with the potential of technological advancements.

Art and creativity are powerful forces, ones that transcend the limitations of digital platforms. The act of creating, whether through painting, writing, music, or other forms of artistic expression, fosters connections that are both deep and enduring. The technology of longing is evident in the ways individuals use digital platforms to share their creations, to create virtual spaces where art and creativity can be celebrated. These creations provide a sense of continuity, fostering connections that are both deep and enduring.

However, the impact of digital platforms on art and creativity is not without challenges. The superficiality of online interactions, the curated nature of social media, and the sense of detachment that often accompanies virtual engagements can create barriers to genuine connection. The technology of longing compels us to navigate these complexities, to find balance between the virtual and the real, and to create spaces where art and creativity can be honored and celebrated. Through this process, we seek to redefine the boundaries of human interaction, to create a future where technology enhances, rather than diminishes, the richness of human connection.

16

Chapter 16: The Power of Music

Music plays a pivotal role in the technology of longing, as individuals seek to navigate the complexities of the digital age. The act of creating and sharing music, the connections it fosters, and the emotions it evokes are essential elements of human interaction. The technology of longing compels us to seek spaces where music can be honored, to find ways to integrate the richness of human experiences with the potential of technological advancements.

Music is a powerful force, one that transcends the limitations of digital platforms. The act of creating and sharing music, whether through composing, performing, or listening, fosters connections that are both deep and enduring. The technology of longing is evident in the ways individuals use digital platforms to share their music, to create virtual spaces where musical experiences can be celebrated. These musical creations provide a sense of continuity, fostering connections that are both deep and enduring.

However, the impact of digital platforms on music is not without challenges. The superficiality of online interactions, the curated nature of social media, and the sense of detachment that often accompanies virtual engagements can create barriers to genuine connection. The technology of longing compels us to navigate these complexities, to find balance between the virtual and the real, and to create spaces where music can be honored and celebrated. Through this process, we seek to redefine the boundaries of human interaction, to create a future where technology enhances, rather than diminishes, the richness of human connection.

17

Chapter 17: The Journey Ahead

The journey ahead is shaped by the technology of longing, as individuals seek to navigate the complexities of the digital age. As technology continues to evolve, the ways in which we connect will be profoundly influenced, reflecting the changing dynamics of human interaction. The technology of longing will drive us to seek meaningful connections, to find balance between virtual and real-life engagements, and to embrace the potential of technological advancements while honoring the depth of human presence.

In the quest for connection, the journey ahead will be marked by moments of nostalgia, solitude, and longing. These emotions will compel us to seek authenticity in our interactions, to navigate the complexities of digital platforms with intentionality and self-awareness. The technology of longing will become a catalyst for deeper human connections, driving us to create spaces where meaningful bonds can be forged.

The journey ahead will be shaped by our ability to reconcile the potential of technology with the essence of human presence. As we navigate this landscape, the technology of longing will remind us of the importance of genuine connections, the joy of shared experiences, and the depth of authentic relationships. Through this process, we will redefine the boundaries of human interaction, seeking to create a future where technology enhances, rather than diminishes, the richness of human connection.

Book Description:

"The Technology of Longing: Nostalgia, Solitude, and the Human Quest for Connection" explores the intricate interplay between technology and human emotion in the digital age. This book delves into the paradoxical nature of modern connectivity, where the advancements meant to bring us closer often amplify our longing for genuine, heartfelt connections. Through seventeen thoughtfully crafted chapters, the book examines the impact of social media, virtual reality, artificial intelligence, and other technological innovations on our quest for intimacy and understanding.

Drawing on the themes of nostalgia and solitude, the book highlights the human desire to reclaim the essence of authentic relationships amidst the cacophony of digital noise. It explores the ways in which individuals navigate the complexities of the digital world, seeking balance between virtual and real-life interactions. The book also emphasizes the role of art, creativity, music, and storytelling in fostering deep and enduring connections.

"The Technology of Longing" is a profound reflection on the human condition in the digital era, offering insights into the challenges and opportunities of modern connectivity. It is a journey through the evolving landscape of human interaction, driven by a timeless yearning for connection, belonging, and the warmth of human presence. Through its exploration of the technology of longing, the book invites readers to embrace the potential of technological advancements while honoring the depth of genuine human connection

www.ingramcontent.com/pod-product-compliance
Lightning Source LLC
LaVergne TN
LVHW020501080526
838202LV00057B/6086